BE STILL *and* KNOW

*One woman's journey of faith amidst
discrimination in the workplace*

Psalm 46:10

DENA RICHARD

Dena Richard

Scripture quotations taken from the Holy Bible: New International Version and King James Version Bible, unless otherwise noted.

Printed in the United States of America

ISBN-13: 9781730723223

Contents

Foreword

As your husband, I have watched you endure heartache and pain through the years. Having to sit back and watch you endure the kind of pain and heartache you endured at the hand of an employer was very difficult for me. Most of the time I would get angry, other times I would just listen, offer support and a strong shoulder to cry on.

As a husband, and a man, you never want to see your wife hurt. Being angry with no real way to let others know just how I really felt wasn't easy, to say the least. Attending work functions with you knowing these were the same individuals mistreating you on a daily basis was the most difficult. Well, as you know, sometimes my facial expression and non-verbal communication would give me away.

I marveled at how you were always able to handle your emotions. One thing you always relied on is your unwavering faith in God and your willingness to listen and obey God's instruction no matter how difficult. You endured write-ups, disciplinary actions, verbal abuse, being overlooked for promotions and increase, as well as many instances of intimidation and scare tactics designed by your employer to make you quit—

all because you were simply standing up for what was right. Most often standing up for your employees and co-workers and not even telling them what was going on.

I would often ask why you wouldn't just leave and your response was always the same, "It's not time." You would also say, "It isn't about me."

You are a strong Christian woman rooted and grounded in the Word of God. "BE STILL AND KNOW" is a testament to God's Word and lets us know His love for us never fails.

Dena, loving you has always been easy for me, but after witnessing what you have gone through, I love you even more because of the selflessness you have shown.

Love,

John

You just never know how strong you are, until strong is all that is left to be. Giving up is NOT an option!

Introduction

God never promised we wouldn't be wrongly accused, persecuted, or treated unfairly. However, He did promise He would never leave us or forsake us (Deuteronomy 31:6). He also promised that no weapon formed against us would prosper (Isaiah 54:17). He even promised that He would be a very present help in times of trouble (Psalm 46:1).

God's Word is full of His promises of deliverance, safety, and refuge. Even better than that, Numbers 23:19 (NLT) reminds us "God is not a man, so He does not lie. He is not human, so He does not change His mind. Has He ever spoken and failed to act? Has He ever promised and not carried it through?"

As my Mom so eloquently puts it, "Not only is God a promise maker, He's a promise keeper." If God is a promise maker, a promise keeper and He doesn't lie, then why is it we continue to stress?

Our job amid all the turmoil and unfairness... "Be still and know that He is God" (Psalms 46:10). Yes, that's it. That's all there is. No magic potions or concoctions. Our job is simply to be still and trust that God has our back. That's easy, right? NOT!

To be still and/or stand still in the face of adversity is no easy feat. I'm not telling you what I heard. I'm telling you what I know. When we are being mistreated, persecuted and falsely accused, our first instinct is to fight back in an effort to vindicate and/or redeem ourselves. Fortunately for us, children of the most high God, our redeemer lives. Fighting back is simply unnecessary.

In fact, fighting back is one of the most detrimental things we can do during this time. If we are in the ring throwing punches, God is not going to risk getting hit (smile). God is a God of order and not confusion. He cannot bless us in that mess and He cannot and will not deliver us in that mess.

We are instructed to "be still and see the salvation of the Lord" (Exodus 14:13; 2 Chronicles 20:17). What does salvation mean? It means *preservation or deliverance from harm, ruin, or loss*. There you have it. That enemy you're fighting in your own strength cannot harm you, cannot ruin you, and cannot cause you to lose anything. God makes sure of it.

Starting to see a trend here? I certainly hope so because trusting in God and standing on these promises will save you countless sleepless nights, heartache and pain.

I spent entirely too much time fighting an enemy God already had His eyes on. God didn't need my help; He needed me to BE STILL. Guess what, God doesn't need your help either.

CHAPTER 1

The "Why"

Let's agree that the devil is pretty clear on his role. It's the devils job to steal, kill and destroy (John 10:10). Steal our hopes and desires; kill our dreams and destroy our destinies before they manifest in the earth in the fullness of God. To do this, the devil must keep us distracted and turn our attention away from fulfilling God's purpose for us.

The devil wants our attention off of God and on the distractions of life and all of its challenges. We can't walk with God fully when we are focused on the problems or challenges before us. Therefore, the devil sends us a little "wind"— that co-worker, boss, friend or family member who is wronging us.

If we walk in bitterness, strife and unforgiveness, or outside the "will of God", we leave room for the enemy to sneak in and destroy us. Our "fight" is with the devil, not man.

Ephesians 6:12 says, "For we wrestle not against flesh and blood, but against principalities, against powers, against rulers of the darkness of this world, against spiritual wickedness in high places."

Sometimes life's challenges can make us forget just how much power we really have in God. The devil knows this too—he used to walk with God daily before he was booted from Heaven. But once you have experienced the true essence of who God is, there is no way you could forget. It is with that knowledge that the devil tries to distract us from walking in our full power.

The devil knows we won't fight him in our own strength but will call on God to help us. The opposite is true when we think we are fighting against a man or woman. We'll take them head-on not praying about or seeking God's guidance about anything. We will take off our shoes *and* earrings (LOL); give them a piece of our minds; clap back; unfriend them on Facebook; and put them on blast on Twitter.

But if that good ole devil shows up, we pray like never before. You can't beat us to church or on our knees. The problem is we don't resist what we don't see. That is why the devil has your eyes on that hateful co-worker, unfair boss or family member and not the actual enemy, which is him. Those individuals are merely there to distract us. God has an out-of-this-world blessing sitting out there waiting for you and the devil must put in work to keep you from getting it. By the way, that blessing is rightfully yours! Just waiting for you to claim it.

The devil is very opportunistic and sneaky. I Peter 5:8 tells us that the devil is like a roaring lion seeking whom he can devour. If you think about the way lions hunt, you will begin to understand what I'm saying here. A lion on the prowl will sit back and patiently watch their prey. They look for the weakest of the pack and those separated from the herd. When we are weak in faith or separated from fellowship with God (leader of the pack/herd) we are prime targets for the devil. The devil knows if we saw a roaring lion headed our way to devour us, we would run away and back to our herd; run back into the fellowship and protection of the leader and protector of the herd (God).

So, think about this... that's why he's hiding behind that hateful co-worker, unfair boss, friend or family member. We're not going to run from them. If anything, we'll plant our feet and prepare for the fight. Like I said, we will take off our shoes *and* earrings. It is then that he gets us to walk in bitterness, unforgiveness and strife—further separating us from God's purpose for our life.

We don't expect to be mistreated, especially not by someone we are close to such as a relative or an intimate partner. When it happens, we experience many emotions including hurt and disappointment. It is at this juncture that many destinies are lost. We become angry and bitter leading us to walk in offense and unforgiveness. Ephesians 4:31-32 clearly instructs us, at length, to:

(31) Get rid of all bitterness, rage, anger, harsh words, and slander, as well as all types of evil behavior. (32) Instead, be kind to each other, tenderhearted, forgiving one another, just as God through Christ has forgiven you.

Why are destines lost and unfulfilled at this juncture? Unforgiveness prevents us from coming into the presence of God. Having unforgiveness causes us to be out of step with God's plan for our life (our destiny). That plan God has to prosper us and not harm us; give us hope and a future (Jeremiah 29:11). That plan God has to do exceedingly, abundantly all we ask or think (Ephesians 3:20). Remember the devil's end game to kill, steal, and destroy mentioned earlier? Steal our hopes and desires; kill our dreams and destroy our destinies before they manifest in the earth in the fullness of God according to God's Word.

CHAPTER 2

The "Why Me"

It's natural to become angry and bitter when someone wrongs us however, it is imperative that we DO NOT. But, rather keep our eyes on God's promises. Just knowing that when we are in alignment with God and walking in love that we have the power to BE STILL and let God fight our battles is enough to shout about right here. That's true power, more power than any co-worker, boss, friend or relative could ever have over you. That's more power than the devil himself will ever have over you.

I'm not telling you what I heard. I'm telling you what I know. For almost two years I fought one of the hardest fights I'd ever fought. I was in a faith fight. Not for my health, as you might be thinking, but for justice and equality. I'm a firm believer in picking my battles and always have.

I'm a nurse by profession and have been for the past 32 years. Over the course of those 32 years, I have witnessed and been the victim of bias and discrimination on various jobs. Discrimination has many forms—race, age, sex, familial status, sexual orientation, religions, disability, etc. The hurt, disappointment and stress it causes is all too real. The discrimination, retaliation and bullying behavior inflicted on workers by some employers has led to those employees committing suicide and homicide.

For the most part we (nurses) don't stick around on jobs where we are mistreated. We don't stay where we are tolerated but rather go where we are celebrated.

Fortunately, in this profession, finding another job is usually easy to do and I'd done so on numerous occasions. I laugh and joke all the time about how nurses are one of the least loyal groups of professionals, meaning we have no problem leaving your company and seeking employment elsewhere if we are mistreated.

This time was different. As badly as I wanted to leave this place, it seemed as if I was somehow being blocked. I applied for several jobs and if I happened to get an interview, it was only so I could later be told someone else had gotten the job. During this time of my job search, I was being lied on, lied to, persecuted, scrutinized, set-up, belittled, demeaned, scolded, overlooked for promotion and advancement... you name it, they were doing it. All because I dared to stand up for what was right. Not because I was a bad employee. As a matter of fact, I was well-respected and revered by my employer until I spoke against wrong-doing and failed to compromise my integrity.

I am no stranger to prayer and God's deliverance. And, since He had delivered me from a similar situation in the past I felt confident He would do so again. I mean He's the same God yesterday, today and tomorrow right?

But, as I stated, this time was different. God seemed to be taking His time and I didn't understand why. I knew God didn't work on our timetable but, He had the power to change things in the blink of an eye so why wasn't he changing this situation for me?

What I didn't realize was that God was working behind the scenes and instantly turning things around for me. Like I said, He and I were on different time schedules and unfortunately His was running a little behind mine (smile). He was lining up people and opportunities that would later cause me to experience promotion and increase. People I didn't know and opportunities I had never dreamed possible would "suddenly" be within my grasp. But, this was all being orchestrated behind the scenes unbeknownst to me. That is why it is so important to continue to walk in love and obedience to God no matter what your situation looks like. It's the only way He can, and will, work "behind the scenes" for us.

When I tell you the devil threw everything he could at me, please believe. It was during this very tumultuous time at work that I learned I would be a grandmother. I am a strong woman of God and the devil knows he can't get me with many of the temptations others may struggle with, such as adultery, drugs, etc. But like all human beings I had my weaknesses.

Please know the devil knows our weaknesses better than we do sometimes. My weakness was my children —my two sons. My husband and I had taught them what my Mom calls "the order". We made confessions over them that they would be Godly men; leaders and not followers; they would be Godly husbands and they would not father children out of wedlock. Well guess what? We were going to be grandparents and not in-laws. And if that was not disappointing enough, since my son was not married, he opted not to tell us but to allow us to see the young lady who, at the time, was around seven or eight months pregnant.

"The order" was no more. "The order" is high school, college, job, wife, house, then babies. Although we were disappointed we opted to see the blessing in the situation. Both he and the mother were adults who were gainfully employed. They were not teenagers who would have to be raised along with their offspring. And... who wouldn't want a grand baby? I heard they call them "grand" for a reason.

Ok, it is what it is, so let's make the best of it and move on, right? Well, not so fast. This is when the real challenge began. Not only was I experiencing persecution on my job, but the young lady and her mother began to lay it on quite thick. I was accused of saying and doing things I had not said or done. I was even threatened by the young ladies' mother. What should have been a happy time, the expectation and delivery of my first grandchild (and a girl at that), turned into a very stressful situation.

I had a few options though. I could be as disrespectful as the two of them were being and give "tit for tat" or I could see them for what they were, a mere distraction, and walk in love knowing God was my redeemer. I decided to do the latter. Those very lengthy, ugly text messages from the young lady were met with a simple "ok" as were the threatening texts from her mother. I had always imagined my sons and their wives calling to tell me they were expecting. I'd always imagined helping plan a baby shower and experiencing the excitement and joy associated with awaiting the birth of my first grandchild, and I was initially somewhat angry that the joy of those experiences had been unfairly taken away from me.

And yes, there were times when the devil said let them have it with both barrels. But, I remembered who I was and whose I was and they simply were not going to get me to stoop to their level. No one was going to pull me away from my "destiny". That devil was not going to steal, kill or destroy anything God had for me. It is important you realize that no one and no thing is worth you walking outside of God's will and not receiving all the good things God has in store for you. Yes, giving each of them a piece of my mind would have felt good, but only momentarily. What I received for not giving them a piece of my mind and walking in love was priceless.

I began to seek God asking what I was doing wrong. What was blocking my blessing? Why was I not able to find a new job and leave that place? Why were this young lady and her mother being so hateful? God could obviously see how badly I was being treated so why didn't He care?

At work I was constantly being told I was not good enough; I didn't have what it took; I needed to take classes; etc. The young lady told me how we portrayed ourselves a loving family but that we really weren't. She essentially called my husband and I "fakes". She accused me of not wanting her to be with my son because she already had a child and was substantially older than my son. Whoa!! This was the one right here that almost got me. I think of all the things she said, that one stung the most.

My mother and biological father divorced when I was less than a year old. My mother remarried a wonderful man, when I was two years old, who loves me as his own. What if he and his family didn't accept my mother because she had me? I would not be the person I am today, nor would I have had the blessing of family that came along with him, loving grandparents, aunts, uncles, and cousins. I would never deny any child the blessing of us.

So not only did her statement hurt me, it made me quite angry. Once again, that ole devil was on his job. I had to look past her statements and count them as mere "distractions". I could not and would not allow anyone or anything to jeopardize my "destiny" and all the goodness God had in store for me.

She deleted me from Facebook, sent Ultrasound pictures to other family members and would not answer her phone when I called. Her mother would text me to tell me "leave my daughter alone or else" shortly thereafter. Why was I being treated so cruel and unfair in what seemed like every area of my life, personal and professional? What was going on???? I know now it was *all* because God had something amazing in store for me and the devil was mad about it.

CHAPTER 3

The "What"

I briefly mentioned knowing who I was and whose I was. Yes, I AM a child of the most high God. I am who God says I am... and so are you. It is so important that we know what God says about us because when we do, it is very difficult for anyone to convince us otherwise.

Like I said, every chance they got, my employer would tell me how I didn't have what it took; how I wasn't good enough; how they had "given" me a job I wasn't worthy of having. They did everything in their power to break me. BUT GOD!!!!

I have never underestimated my value or my worth. I have never possessed low self-esteem and I know I'm smart. I am who God says I am, and so are you.

Eleanor Roosevelt once said, "No one can make you feel inferior without your consent." She was right. You have what you allow and hurting people hurt other people. Misery loves company and bottom line is some people are so messed up in their minds with insecurities and self-esteem issues that when they see someone who is confident, they start trying to make that person feel inferior to make themselves feel better.

Stop allowing individuals to speak inferiority and defeat over you. Why do you believe the lies of those employers, family members and friends, and don't believe the truth in God's Word?

God tells us who we are throughout the Bible. Try taking God at His word and stop listening to the voice of those whose intent is on destroying you. God says we are: Fearfully and wonderfully made (Psalm 139:14). "Wonderful" is defined as *admirable or very good; excellent or splendid. Capable of eliciting wonder; astonishing*.

That employer who tried to convince me that I wasn't good enough had no idea who they were dealing with (smile). I knew they had to look UP to me when they said it because the inferiority issues were theirs and not mine. Those individuals who are attempting to beat you down must look UP to you as well. We elicit wonder in them. They find us astonishing (big smile).

Protected - (Psalm 121: 1-8) - What the enemy didn't realize is that being a child of the most high God also comes with the benefit of protection. See, my Father was not going to allow me to slip. He kept watch over me, keeping me from *all* hurt. There was no way they could ever hurt me. Therefore, it is so important that we know who we are; what benefits we have as believers and how to walk in faith knowing God is not a man that He would lie or fail. He hasn't failed me yet. He hasn't failed you either.

Prosperous - Jeremiah 29:11 says "For I know the thoughts that I think toward you, says the Lord, thoughts of peace and not of evil, to give you a future and a hope." Ephesians 3:20 says "Now to Him who is able to do exceedingly abundantly above all that we ask or think, according to the power that works in us." John 3:2 says "Beloved, I wish above all things that thou mayest prosper and be in health, even as thy soul prospers."

"Prosper" is defined as *success in material terms; be financially successful; flourish physically; grow strong and healthy.* Lord these folks fooled around and let me discover who I was and my birth rights (LOL). God says we have peace and not evil. He says we are entitled to "exceedingly abundantly" above all we could ask or think. He said we are successful financially, flourish physically and grow strong and healthy. So, *they* could not deny me a promotion, raise or increase.

In the natural it looked like they did all of those things, BUT GOD! See, God is a God of promotion and increase and He has a way of not only providing promotion and increase He will also "catch you up". God will give you double for your trouble; restore you and cause you to be ahead of where you were when you were wronged. I'm not telling you what I heard, I'm telling you what I know. Just look a Job and how God not only restored him but gave him double.

BORN TO WIN - Romans 8:37 says, "we are more than conquerors…". "Conquer" is defined as *to successfully overcome (a problem or weakness).* 2 Corinthians 2:14 says God always causes us to triumph. "Triumph" is defined as *a great victory or achievement*. Notice how God always causes us to have the victory. That means we win every time. When I became born again and joined the family of believers, winning became my "birthright", therefore I am BORN TO WIN.

I recall taking a piece of paper and writing "BORN TO WIN" on it and taping it to my computer screen. I firmly believe in speaking positive things over myself and my loved ones. This time I made my enemies speak positive things over me as well. What's funny is they had no idea that every time they walked past my desk, scoffed at my note and said it aloud they were speaking my "WIN". I'm quite confident that note was the topic of many closed-door conversations among my employers, but every time they said, "she's BORN TO WIN", in reference to me, regardless of their sarcasm they were pushing me toward a victory.

God said in His word that He would make our enemies our foot stool (Psalm 110:1) I put my feet on their backs and rested. I believe "use what you got", so they got used (LOL). Also, foot stools are used UNDER your feet therefore you enemies are UNDER your feet. What are the soles of your feet used for, to walk on correct? Walk on your enemies by writing their names on the bottoms of your shoes (LOL). You need to know your enemy's worth as well, I'm just saying (smile).

Untouchable - (Romans 8:1) - God said no weapon formed against me would prosper. He didn't say they wouldn't "form" but He did say they wouldn't prosper. A gentleman by the name of M.C. Hammer wrote a song "Can't touch this". That song would come to mind every time I was in the presence of my employer and they were trying to belittle me and talk down to me. I know there were times we met that they thought I was insane. I started smiling so much when they did it, they started to get aggravated. They were forging weapons against me that were no good and I knew they were fighting a battle they couldn't win. They were wronging me and many just like me. I was standing up for what was right and God had no choice but to honor that. It doesn't matter what people call you, it only matters what YOU answer to.

Some people and even employers are confident in their ability to make others feel inferior because they have done so, and been allowed to do so, so many times in the past. Unfortunately, the world is full of insecure, intimidated individuals who feel they must destroy you to elevate them. But... every now and then they will "meet their match" and encounter a child of the Most High God they cannot and will not shake. Why? Because we are BORN TO WIN!!!

I wasn't doing anything wrong; there wasn't anything wrong with me; I had every skill and talent needed to perform any task; I was a good person with a kind and loving heart. It was simply the enemies' desire to get into my mind, mess me up, and cause me to think I was not good enough. The mind is a very powerful thing and many battles have been fought, won and lost in a person's mind.

Being who I am causes me to see the good in everyone. I could easily say that's not a good trait, given what I've been through, but I wouldn't dare change who I am based on the actions of few hurting individuals. And neither should you. Just know that hurt people, hurt people, or at least try to. Your job is to pray for them and keep it moving. Don't allow them to be distractions sent to steal, kill and destroy your joy.

Believe me when I tell you God kept me. Without a shadow of doubt, I know it was God. I could not have made it through everything the enemy threw at me had it not been for God. I had to trust Him totally and I had to be obedient. That obedience demanded I be still. The very thing that is so hard to do in the face of adversity. I couldn't fight back. I knew I was right and I was doing the right thing but I couldn't fight back.

The most difficult thing I had to do was BE STILL. My destiny depended on me being still.

I'm an only child with an alpha personality who has no problem fighting for what I believe is right. It was a process, to say the least but, there was no denying what I read in Hebrews 13:5 (Amplified Bible Version)... for He has said, "I will never [under any circumstances] desert you [nor give you up nor leave you without support, nor will I in any degree leave you helpless], nor will I forsake or let you down or relax My hold on you [assuredly not]!"

It was during one of my therapy sessions that, for the very first time, I realized what my purpose was and why I was going through this. It would be my testimony that would help someone else going through a similar situation. A testimony of how *I* overcame.

Prior to this experience, I never thought I had a "credible" testimony. What do I mean? Well, I've never been drunk; I've never used drugs; I've never smoked marijuana; I've never been abused; I've never been hungry or homeless; I've never been promiscuous; I've never had a child out of wedlock; I've never committed adultery; I am heterosexual; I'm not a liar; I'm not a cheater; I'm not a thief; I'm not a murderer; and I've even been called a "goody two shoes". I had no "street cred".

Most of the powerful testimonies I've ever heard or seen on social media or in main stream media had to do with an individual, or individuals, being delivered from at least one of these challenges. So, what exactly was I going to testify having been delivered from or having overcome? A STOLEN DESTINY!

I "overcame" and was "delivered" from the devil's attempts to steal, kill and destroy. Steal my hopes and desires; kill my dreams and destroy my destiny before they manifest in the Earth in the fullness of God according to God's Word. That's what!! That's my testimony.

That thing the devil was working so hard to keep me from was this book. A book that exposes his plans to steal, kill and destroy. That is why the devil was fighting me so hard. That is why he is fighting so many of you right now. It looks as if your world is falling apart and everything that can go wrong is going wrong. You feel like you are at the end of your rope. God says "NO". Tie a knot in the end of that rope and hold on. STAY THE COURSE!!! Many of you are in your "Midnight Hour". It is in that "midnight hour" that breakthroughs happen and the power of God is manifested.

"But about midnight Paul and Silas were praying and singing hymns of praise to God and the prisoners were listening to them; and suddenly there came a great earthquake, so that the foundations of the prison house were shaken; and immediately all the doors were opened and everyone's chains were unfastened" (Acts 16). At midnight, God set the captives free.

Paul and Silas were Godly men who loved God and shared His gospel. During their time in Philippi, people were saved and the church was established. The devil of course was not happy. They did nothing wrong but were arrested, beaten and put in prison for their preaching. They did not fight back and they did not walk in bitterness, strife and unforgiveness as the devil would have liked. They knew they need only be still and see the salvation of the Lord. They were so confident in God's power they praised God right in the midst of their trial.

If you really want to make the devil mad, praise God when you have tied a knot in that rope and are holding on for dear life. God will honor your faith and deliver you from the midst of your enemies. Your enemies will be in awe of God's power. Many ungodly men/women have turned their lives around and joined the Family of Believers after having seen God's children delivered from what seemed like impossible circumstances.

This passage of scripture (Read Acts 16:25-34) goes on to say, when the jailer awoke and saw the prison doors opened, he drew his sword and was about to kill himself, supposing that the prisoners had escaped. But Paul cried out with a loud voice saying, "Do not harm yourself, for we are all here". He (the jailer) called for lights and rushed in, and trembling with fear he fell down before Paul and Silas.

After he brought them out, he said Sirs what must I do to be saved? They said, "Believe in the Lord Jesus and you will be saved, you and your household". And they spoke the Word of the Lord to him together with all who were in his house. And he took them that very hour of the night and washed their wounds, and immediately he was baptized, he and his entire household.

I've also read other accounts where several of their fellow prisoners were also saved that night. The devil was defeated and once again God prevailed. Paul and Silas' destinies were not stolen. They were not distracted by persecution and wrong doing. They went on to Thessalonica and preached to a synagogue of Jews and some of the Jews were also saved. Many lives were changed because of Paul and Silas and the devil knows many lives will be changed because of you and me when we fulfill our God given destinies.

It is in that midnight hour we need to take care not to allow our destinies to be stolen. It is in that darkest hour that we throw in the towel and give up; we get off course. Our destinies, as well as the destinies of people we don't even know, depend on us *not* giving up.

CHAPTER 4

Trust

Yes, it was a process. First, I had to TRUST God. No problem there. I knew He's a rewarder of those who diligently seek Him. He and I had history (LOL). I was good. I had no issues or reservations about trusting God, and had done so many times and had even faced times when I couldn't do anything except trust God.

The Bible is very clear and full of biblical content and scriptures related to trusting God. One need only Google it. Look what Joshua 1:9 tells us, "Have I not commanded you? Be strong and courageous. Do not be afraid; do not be discouraged, for the Lord your God will be with you wherever you go." These two right here got me through some tough times, Psalms 56:3, "When I am afraid, I put my trust in you" and Proverbs 3:5-6 "Trust in the Lord with all your heart and lean not on your own understanding. In all your ways submit to Him, and He will make your paths straight." I especially turned to Proverbs 3:5-6 when I didn't know which direction to go.

There are so many others, Psalm 31:14; 2 Samuel 7:28; Psalm 9:10; Psalm 13:5; Psalm 84:12; Daniel 6:23; and the list goes on. Speaking of Daniel 6:23, who wouldn't trust a God who could close a hungry lion's mouth and cause him not to eat you? And, let's not forget Daniel 3:27. Who goes into a fire and comes out without smelling like smoke?

One of many things God spoke to me during this ordeal was Daniel 3:27. God assured me I "would come through the fire and not smell like smoke". Let me give you a little background here.

In the Bible, King Nebuchadnezzar became angry when three Hebrew boys, Shadrach, Meshach and Abed-nego refused to serve his gods and worship a golden idol he set before them. The King ordered the three young men be placed inside a furnace to be burned to death. We see in Daniel 3:24 where the

King looked into the furnace after having placed the three inside and said, "Did we not throw three men who were tied up into the midst of the fire"? The King was correct. They had indeed thrown three bound men into the furnace. What astonished the King was that he now saw four men untied, walking around in the midst of the fire who were not hurt (Daniel 3:25).

God spoke Daniel 3:27 into my spirit during my ordeal to let me know that although I was thrown into a fire meant to destroy me, He would deliver me and I would not be touched. "I wouldn't even smell like smoke". Who wouldn't trust a God who could do that? Daniel 3:27 reads "The satraps, the prefects, the governors and the king's counselors gathered around them and saw that regarding these men the fire had no effects on their bodies. Their hair was not singed, their clothes were not scorched or damaged, and even the smell of smoke was not on them".

They were "untouched" and "unbothered". They stood still and trusted God and the reward was great. Nebuchadnezzar recognized and acknowledged the "God of Shadrach, Meshach, and Abed-nego" and he caused Shadrach, Meshach, and Abed-nego to prosper in Babylon (Daniel 3 28:30).

I would be remiss if I didn't include the story my Mom kept before me during my trials; the story of

Jehoshaphat and his army. 2 Chronicles tells us how Jehoshaphat cried out to God when an enemy of great multitude was coming against him and his people (2 Chronicles 20:5-6, 12). Two armies had joined forces to come against them. During my adversity I noticed how my enemies were joining forces to destroy me as well. In the natural there was no way Jehoshaphat and his followers would be able to defeat such great armies in battle. In the natural there was no way I could defeat the enemies coming against me as they were great in number and great in authority over me.

A victory in each of these situations could only come from God. And, just like Jehoshaphat, I knew this and knew my trust had to be in God. Jehoshaphat said "…. we do not know what to do, but our eyes are on you" (2 Chronicles 20:12). We later see in the chapter where Jehoshaphat is assured he and his army would not have to fight. All they had to do was stand still and see the salvation of the Lord. Sound familiar? "You need not fight in this battle; take your positions, stand and witness the salvation of the Lord who is with you, O Judah and Jerusalem. Do not fear or be dismayed; tomorrow go out against them, for the Lord is with you" (2 Chronicles 20:17).

As powerful as this is, hold on to your hats, there's more. Jehoshaphat and his army went down to meet their enemies singing and praising God. We need not wait until our battle is over to shout. We can shout now! If God has assured you of a victory you can rest on it. He is not a man and He does not lie. Not only did God deliver Jehoshaphat and his army, He caused the other armies to turn on each other. They destroyed each other.

How many of us have had people gang up on us in an attempt to destroy us then notice those individuals were soon at odds with each other? Jehoshaphat and his army did not have to lift a finger against their enemies and neither do we. All we should do is stand still, stand still and see the salvation and deliverance of the Lord. All the time, God was working in the background devising a plan to provide promotion and increase. After those armies destroyed each other all their possessions were up for grabs. God instructed Jehoshaphat and his people to collect those riches. The amount of equipment, garments, precious jewels and metals left behind by those armies was so great it took Jehoshaphat and his people three days to carry away all those valuables. Trusting in God not only gets you the victory, it gets you exceedingly and abundantly above all you could ask or think. God always puts you in a place better than you were before. He is faithful. He will give you beauty for your ashes.

Whether you believe it or not people are watching you. If you talk about trusting God but are always worried and bothered, you are not truly trusting God. Just like Nebuchadnezzar saw the trust Shadrach, Meshach, and Abed-nego had in their God and how their God delivered them; and just how we saw God cause Jehoshaphat's army to defeat a mighty enemy without lifting a finger, others need to see the trust we have in our God and how He delivers us. This is how we bring others into fellowship with God. After all, remember the world believes, "Seeing is believing" and "talk is cheap".

CHAPTER 5

Faith

Secondly, I had to have FAITH in God. No problem
here. I knew He's not a man and would not lie. I knew
He's faithful to do what He says He'll do. Once again,
He and I had history and I was good. My faith walk
was strong. I was willing to say "God, I don't know
when You are going to do it or how You're going to do
it, but I trust You enough to believe You are going to
do it." That's faith.

I didn't say it was easy nor did I say I didn't have
my moments. The Bible is clear when it comes to us
having faith in God. Mark 10:52 illustrates Jesus'

instructions to a blind man after Jesus restored his sight "Go, your faith has healed you." This man was Bartimaeus and he had been blind since birth. Bartimaeus cried out to Jesus as He was passing by despite others around him telling him to be quiet.

Sometimes we must speak up. We must go out there and put our faith on the line despite what our family and friends might be saying. After all, our blessing is at stake not theirs. I've heard several people say, "a closed mouth doesn't get fed." Well Bartimaeus decided that day he was going to be fed. He received his sight immediately and began to follow Jesus, much to the dismay of those who had tried to discourage him.

This sort of thing happens every day. That is why it's best sometimes to keep your visions, dreams and plans to yourself. Not everyone in the boat with you is rowing the same way you are. The hardest thing is when you realize the person who wholeheartedly believes for your failure is your family member or friend. BUT GOD!! He always causes us to triumph.

I didn't read John 11:40 until I was doing research for this book but and as I was writing this all I could say was "GLORY TO GOD". John 11:40 reads "Then Jesus said, did I not tell you that if you believe you will see the glory of God?"   This one verse could possibly change your life.

The Bible describes faith as confidence in what we hope for and assurance about what we do not see (Hebrews 11:1).   If you're stuck in "seeing is believing" mode here you might want to renew your mind because true faith is "believing without seeing".

It took an act of faith for Moses to lead the people of Israel through the Red Sea (Exodus 14:13-14). "Moses told the people, fear not; stand still and see the salvation of the Lord which He will work for you today. For the Egyptians you have seen today, you shall never see again. The Lord will fight for you, and you shall hold your peace and remain at rest."

There it is again, that same promise, "stand still and see God's salvation". No fighting necessary!! God may not come when we want Him, but He's always on time.

I became weary. I was tired of being beat up on. It seemed as if the enemy's attacks were becoming more frequent and more vicious. Just as I was about to give up (my midnight), I can remember seeing one of them walk by my desk and God spoke to me as clear as day, "The Egyptian you see today, you will see no more." That was the last time I saw that individual. Shortly after that incident God delivered me from the situation. That one word from God provided the strength I needed in that moment to forge ahead knowing that my deliverance was nigh.

Just like He did for the children of Israel, God showed Himself faithful and delivered me out of the hands of my enemies. So many times, we give up too soon. If I had given up that day, I would have missed all the blessings God had in store for me on the other side of that ordeal. I had to show myself faithful as well and so do you. It's always darkest before midnight, but tie a knot in your rope and hold on. STAY THE COURSE!!!!

Our blessings are for an appointed time and the devil knows when that time is. He really starts coming against us when he knows we're on the verge of our breakthrough. Know that when it seems like all hell is breaking loose and everything and everybody is coming against you, God is about to do something miraculous for you. Stay in Faith and don't give up! Feed your spirit with the Word of God.

Remember the story I told you earlier about Paul and Silas? We read in Acts 16 where at midnight Paul and Silas prayed, and sang praises unto God and the prisoners heard them. And how suddenly there was a great earthquake came and the shook the prison causing the prison doors to immediately open and every prisoner's shackles be loosed. Paul and Silas had been arrested, beaten and thrown into jail unjustly. In their darkest hour, midnight, they prayed.   Those prayers not only caused God to suddenly work for them, but for every prisoner.   Two words caught my eye, "suddenly" and "immediately".   Paul and Silas praised God despite their circumstances.

It's hard to pray during these times and God knows this. Therefore, it is so important for us to "sacrifice praise".   What do I mean?   "Sacrifice" is defined as, *surrendering a possession; something given up or lost.* "Praise" is defined as, *express warm approval or admiration of; commend; applaud.* Paul and Silas were in prison so I doubt very seriously if they were in a state of approval or admiration. But, they did have the ability to surrender and give up something—their praises. Their destinies depended on them doing so.

When God has blessed, protected and even vindicated us it is very easy for us to feel generous toward Him. We will openly offer up praise and thanksgiving during those times. It doesn't cost us anything at that point. But in those times when God doesn't show up when we want—we get a bad medical report, or our child is lost—God seems far from us and the last thing we feel like doing is praising Him. To praise God in those times requires sacrifice. We must do it anyway, regardless of our circumstances.

In the previous chapters I've given examples of how God delivered His people out of circumstances no one thought was possible. Well, He said in Malachi 3:6, "For I am the Lord, I do not change." So, He'll do the same thing for you and I.

During one of my therapy sessions, my therapist could obviously see the ordeal I was going through was beginning to take a toll on me both physically and mentally. She suggested I listen to a song by Casting Crowns called "Praise Him in the Storm". I'd never heard of this group or this song, but I was willing to listen. I listened to this song that night and I began to praise God in my storm. I began to praise Him despite my circumstances. The song went something like this: "I was sure by now, God you would have reached down and wiped our tears away. Stepped in and saved the day....... And I'll praise you in this storm; And I will lift my hands; That you are who you are; No matter where I am; And every tear I've cried; You hold in your hand; You never left my side; And though my heart is torn; I will praise you in this storm".

I had to "sacrifice praise".

CHAPTER 6

Listen

Next, I had to LISTEN. I recognized God's voice. I knew everything from Him is good and very good. I knew Jesus came that we might have life and have it more abundantly. So, anything contrary to this I knew was not from God. That's low-level stuff though. What I soon discovered, as this ordeal unfolded, I was hearing God on a higher level. He was warning me of impending attacks from the enemy like impromptu meetings, report and document request days in advance of the enemy's actual request. He didn't let anything sneak up on me. He was protecting me. Those impromptu meetings with those document request designed to set me up and produce grounds to get rid of me soon became folly at the hand of my God.

Everything the enemy said I wasn't doing or didn't have the skill to do was set before him in complete order proving him wrong time and time again. The enemy left those impromptu meetings "confounded and confused". I began to see their frustration. My faith and my constitution became stronger and I knew God was fighting for me.

With respect to my son's situation (see Chapter 2), God told me to just be quiet and only speak or say something when He told me to do so. He also instructed me to "remove myself" which meant I had to in turn block the calls/text messages and social media feeds. God was protecting me once again. He was not allowing me to walk in strife and unforgiveness.   He was protecting me from "distractions".

We must be able to hear from God. He's not just going to open the heavens and call us out. LOL!! Some people describe it as a "still, small voice".   Some people describe as a "gut feeling" and some describe it as "peace". However you describe it, God has a way of speaking to each of us. It's up to us to be in position to hear Him when He does.

What do I mean? For God to speak to us we must be willing to listen. He can speak to us in many ways. The most common is through His word. Read your Bible. It's God's blueprint for life. It helps you to understand the nature of God, His promises and His rewards.

People say all the time "if it's God's will". What do you mean "IF"? There is no excuse not to know God's will for your life, it's in the Bible. You don't have to say, "I'll get well if it's God's will." It is His will, He told you in the Bible. Just like the nature of the devil is revealed, the nature of God is also revealed in John 10:10, "The thief comes only to steal and kill and destroy; I have come that they may have life, and have it to the full". "Full" in this scripture means *containing or holding as much or as many as possible; having no empty space.*

God adds and multiplies; the devil subtracts and divides. So, the next time you say God took something or someone from you, think again. It's not in His nature. The next time you preface a statement with "If it's God's will", remember God's nature. And yes... He means full in every area of your life. Full in your health, full in your finances, full in your relationships, full in your mind and spirit.

Another way God speaks to us is through other people. This is where it becomes imperative that you know God's nature and study God's Word for yourself. If someone comes up to you and says these words "God told me to tell you...." you should be in listening mode. Listen first to make sure what they are saying lines up with God's nature and His word (THE BIBLE). If it doesn't, God didn't send that person to you. Yes, just like that, I'm saying they are lying to you.

Secondly, listen for confirmation. God will tell you something first and then have someone else tell you the same thing or "confirm" what He already spoke to you. This is helpful when you are struggling with the uncertainty of what you believe God may have said to you regarding a certain prayer or request.

One day, as I was going through the ordeal on my job, I asked God if I was doing what I should be doing and if He was with me. A few days later as I was coming out of Bath and Body Works, with my never-ending supply of stress relief aromatherapy oils and candles, a stranger approached me. She was an older lady and I initially thought she wanted to know if I had some extra coupons. Instead she smiled and said, "I don't know you and I don't even know what this means, but I just heard God tell me to tell you 'yes'. " When she saw the look on my face she said, "Do you know what that means?" All I could say, past the tears in my eyes, "Yes ma'am, I asked God a question a few days ago."

She proceeded to tell me how God told her to tell me this when she saw me coming out the store, and how she had ignored the feeling initially, but when she touched the door handle to enter the store she heard it even louder. She said she knew then she'd better say something. I am so thankful for her ability to listen to God as well as her obedience to God. That one word from God provided the strength I needed in that moment to forge ahead knowing that I was doing what God wanted me to do, and even more importantly, that He was with me. Having that assurance also let me know that God was going to do everything He needed to do on my behalf. I could be still.

God also speaks to us directly. That's what I described earlier when I mentioned how God would warn me of impromptu meetings and impending request for documents and reports. During this ordeal God started speaking to me (no it wasn't audible) as soon as I got out of bed. He would speak to me while my family was still sleeping and before the distractions of my day began. My mind was rested and He had my full attention.

This began to happen daily so I started leaving a pen and pad on my dresser. There was not a day that went by that God didn't prepare me for the attack of the enemy. As a matter of fact, my husband noticed how I would get out of bed and write something every day. He finally asked what I wrote every morning. I told him I was writing down what God said I would need for the day. He never questioned my answer, but merely smiled.

Lastly, God gives us what I like to call "pause". "Pause" is *a temporary stop in action or speech*. There are times when God will nudge or prompt us to stop doing something or to stop saying something. I also refer to this as "not having peace". Peace is defined as "freedom from disturbance; quiet; calm; restful".

I have learned to pause when I don't have peace. If I don't feel calm about it or I am somehow disturbed by it, don't get mad if I tell you "NO", because for me if I don't have peace, it's a N.O. to infinity and beyond. You're not going to make me do it. And, if I'm your Mom, you're not doing it either (LOL).

Several years ago, my sons asked if they could go to one of those trampoline parks. I initially said yes, signed the on-line release forms and had every intention of sending them on their way. They also had one of their friends with them. They were in the car and had gotten to the end of the driveway when the most disturbing feeling came over me. I felt they didn't need to go. I went outside and stopped the car making them come back into the house. My oldest son and his friend got out of the car, without a word, came into the house and started playing video games. My youngest son was very upset and verbalized his displeasure with what I had done. He asked, why? I told him I didn't know why. I didn't have a reason for him, only that I didn't have peace. I also explained that the lack of peace and uneasiness did not come over me until he had gotten into the car.

I didn't have that feeling when my oldest son and his friend were in the car. It was my youngest who didn't need to go. That uneasiness was somehow tied to my youngest son. It would have been perfectly fine for my oldest son and his friend to go to the trampoline park, and leave my youngest behind. I later asked my oldest son why he calmly exited the car and did not provide push-back like his younger brother. He simply said, "You've done me like that before and usually something happens so I'm used to it."

To my amazement, when I opened the newspaper the following day, there was a 20-something year old young man in a wheelchair, paralyzed from his neck down after a spinal cord injury he received during a visit to one of those trampoline parks. The article went on and on about how unsafe and under-regulated those parks were. Several well-known orthopedic specialists stated how dangerous the parks were and how they and some of their colleagues were working on legislation to close such parks. You know I showed this article to little Mr. Unhappy (LOL!). Little Mr. Unhappy, the daredevil, would have most likely pushed the envelope and taken chances he shouldn't have, causing injury or even death. That is why my uneasy feeling was tied to him and not the other boys.

I know we have busy lives, but it is so important we are in tune to God and His messages. It could be the difference between life and death. How many of us have been heading somewhere and get delayed, only to later discover there was a car accident or some other tragedy along the route we were planning to take? And, the accident or tragedy happened at precisely the time we would have been there had it not been for that delay. Well, not only will God cause a delay to protect us, He will speak to us with instructions that also protect us. Something to think about, huh???

LISTEN!!!!

CHAPTER 7

Obey

I had to OBEY. Obedience is better than sacrifice. Yes, I could have gone into those meetings and really shown them a thing or two (LOL), but that's not what God said to do. He told me which documents to present, which reports to provide, what to say and what not to say. I had to listen and obey Him.

There were times when I was about to provide too much information and God would tell me to remove items. There were times when I really wanted to tell them exactly what I thought, but God would bridle my tongue. Did I always obey? I would like to say I did, but that would be a lie. And since God gives us free will, I went off script several times.

Sometimes I took what I wanted to take to those meetings and sometimes I said what I wanted to say at those meetings. Remember what I said in the introduction? I spent entirely too much time fighting an enemy God already had His eyes on. God didn't need my help; He needed me to be still. Thank You, Lord for grace and mercy, in spite of my disobedience!

The Bible is very clear when it comes to being obedient. God tells us in John 14:15, "If you love me, you will keep my commandments." If we love God, we will be obedient to His will. Why is our obedience so important to God? Our obedience to Him proves our love for Him and demonstrates our faith in Him.

Israel's history shows that the biggest problem of God's covenant people was their repeated failure to obey God's commands. God always blessed their obedience, but their propensity for disobedience caused them great misery and their eventual demise.

This is true in our lives as well. God is clear in His requirement for His people. Deuteronomy 10:12-15 states, "And now, Israel, what does the Lord your God require from you, but to fear the Lord your God, to walk in all His ways and to love Him, and to serve the

Lord your God with all your heart and with all your soul, and to keep the commandments of the Lord and His statutes which I am commanding you today for your good? Behold, the heavens belong to the Lord your God, the earth and all that is in it. Yet the Lord had a delight in loving your fathers and set His affection on them, and He chose their descendants after them, you above all people, as it is this day."

It's clear—we are to obey God for our own good. The Bible is full of stories about individuals who habitually disobeyed God's will. Saul is one of those individuals. You can read about Saul's disobedience in 1 Samuel, chapter 15.

God sent the prophet Samuel to Saul with the message that Saul would be King of Israel and God wanted him to destroy the Amalekites. Saul was instructed to destroy everything. He was not to spare man, woman, child, infant or any livestock. Everything and everyone was to be destroyed.

However, Saul did not obey God's instruction, but instead decided to capture Agag, the king of the Amalekites, alive and spare the best of the livestock. Saul's disobedience caused God to regret ever having made Saul king over Israel. Saul rejected God's instructions, God rejected Saul as king and another king was selected, David. Saul became jealous of

David and spent many years plotting to kill David, but the Lord protected him. David found favor with the Lord. Saul did not. Saul later lost his life in battle.

Just as the Bible is full of stories of individuals who disobeyed God's commands, it contains multiple accounts of individuals who obeyed God's commands and reaped the blessings thereof. One of those individuals was Abraham.

In the 22nd chapter of Genesis, Abraham was prepared to sacrifice his only child, Isaac, as God commanded. How many of us, with more than one child, would be willing to sacrifice any of our children if God asked? If you read the entire account, you will see that God did not allow Abraham to harm Isaac but rather provided a ram for the sacrifice. It was a test of Abraham's obedience.

God's response to Abraham's obedience is also revealed in Genesis 22:16-18, "By Myself I have sworn, declares the Lord, that since you have done this thing and have not withheld your son, your only son, indeed I will greatly multiply your descendants like the stars of the heavens and like the sand on the seashore; and your seed shall possess the gate of their enemies. Through your seed all the nations of the earth shall be blessed, because you have heard and obeyed My voice."

Wow, Abraham started with no descendants; got out of the will of God (Genesis 16); got back in God's will; and God gave him more descendants than stars in heaven (Genesis 22).   God is serious about this obedience thing!   And.... His blessings for those who obey Him!

Just like Abraham, my obedience was directly tied to my blessing. And, just like Abraham and I, your obedience is directly tied to your blessing as well.

We must be obedient and seek God even when we might think we have something under control and don't need God's help.

We see in 2 Samuel 5 where David inquired of God if to fight the Philistines. "So, David inquired of the lord, saying, Shall I go up against the Philistines? Will you deliver them into my hand? The Lord responded in that same verse with "Go up, for I will doubtless deliver the Philistines into your hand." So, David did as the Lord instructed, proceeded into battle and defeated the Philistines.

I specifically wanted to mention this passage of scripture because there's a special lesson in it for us all. See, this is not the only time David inquired of the Lord if he should enter into battle with the Philistines. In verse 23 we see where David consults the Lord again for the same thing. Verse 23 and 24 read: Therefore David inquired of the Lord, and He said, "you shall not go up; circle around behind them, and come upon them in front of the mulberry tree. And it shall be, when you hear marching in the tops of the mulberry trees, and then you shall advance quickly. For then the Lord will go out before you to strike the camp of the Philistines." Once again David did as the Lord commanded him and defeated the Philistines.

Why is there a special lesson in this story for us? Because David did not get comfortable in his own might. He did not take for granted that he had defeated the same enemy in the past and assumed it was a fight he needed to undertake, if for no other reason than he knew he could win. Remember this is the same person who as a teenager defeated a lion, a bear, and a giant. He consulted God. His trust was totally in God. He did not consider his own strength. This time, like the previous time, God allowed David to prevail. Had David not consulted God, like so many of us fail to do, he would have most likely lost the battle or had a very difficult time defeating his enemy.

Why do we continue time after time to make things so hard for ourselves? Humble yourselves and consult God. He tells us in His Word that His yoke is easy and

His burdens are light, yet we continuously prefer the hard yoke and heavy burdens.

You can find scriptures related to obedience from Genesis to Revelations; each with its own promise and blessing from God.

Be Obedient!!!

CHAPTER 8

Be Still

Now for the big one, I had to BE STILL. For almost two years, God kept Psalm 46:10 before me. He spoke it in my quiet time. He spoke it during those challenging times when I was being lied on, persecuted and falsely accused.

He spoke it in those impromptu meetings. He constantly instructed me to be still. Be still and know that He is God. Be still and see His salvation. All I needed to do was be still, He was fighting the battle. The very battle He chose. I did not choose this battle.

After all, who chooses to be placed in an uncomfortable and adverse situation?

God saw the injustice long before I did and, as my mom so eloquently put it, one evening when I was about to give up, "every now and then God raises up individuals to fight for what is right." When your Mom throws something like that out there and gives you examples like David (in the Bible) and Dr. Martin Luther King, Jr., you tend to stop your pity party and forge ahead.

When God grants you grace and mental toughness, you are a force to be reckoned with. But when God gives you grace, mental toughness AND a praying mother, you become unstoppable! If God brings you to it, He will bring you through it. And... that He did!

We see numerous examples throughout the Bible of individuals who were up against what seemed like unsurmountable odds and circumstances. Yet God delivered them; and not only caused them to triumph, but caused their circumstances to become better than they could have ever imagined.

Well I'm not in the Bible, but I am one of those individuals. I endured a lot during those two years. Things I have not told anyone, including my husband. Only God and those who persecuted me know the lies that were told, the plots that were devised, and the desire they had to destroy me.

What I didn't realize at the time was the only thing that really mattered was that God knew. He saw and heard everything they did to me, said to me, and said about me. God knew my heart and He knew theirs. And I knew Romans 8:31: What then shall we say to all these things? If God is for us, who can be against us?

The answer is no one and no thing. Why was God with me and not with them? Like I said, He knew my heart and He knew theirs. They'd already lost when they came against me the first time. It just took me almost two years to realize this. And, it took me almost two years to be still so God could fight the battle.

My lack of knowledge coupled with bouts of disobedience caused my deliverance to be delayed. I don't desire this for you. God does not desire this for you. To whom much is given, much is required. God has given me much and He requires much of me. He placed it in my heart to write this book to share my ordeal and ultimate deliverance with you, so your deliverance will not be delayed unnecessarily. I can't tell you everything that went on during those two years. I can't even elaborate on the outcome but I will say....

Now thanks be unto God, which always causes us to triumph in Christ, and make manifest the savor of his knowledge by us in every place (2 Corinthians 2:14).

I often think of Job (in the Bible, Book of Job) and how the devil took everything from him. He took his children, his wealth, and his health. The Bible says that Job was a just man and walked upright before God. The devil desired to destroy him and believed the only reason Job was serving God was because of his many blessings. Like I mentioned earlier, God knows our hearts. God knew Job would serve Him no matter what circumstances came Job's way.

Can God say the same about us? Unfair circumstances happen to us all. Life happens to us all. Our actions are what will ultimately determine our deliverance, not the actions of others. Job's actions not only lead to his deliverance but to his restoration and increase as well. Job received more from God than he had prior to his trial. Job's latter end was more than his beginning.

God blessed him with long life and, although Job lost his children in the beginning, he was blessed with more children—God allowed Job to see four generations (Job 42).

Be Still!!!

CHAPTER 9

Forgive

Ok, so I placed my trust in God; I maintained faith in God; I listened to God; I obeyed God; and I was being still in the face of adversity and persecution. Why hadn't God stepped in to deliver me from this situation?

God hadn't stepped in because I was pissed, for lack of a better term. How dare these people treat me the way they were treating me?! I was being openly mistreated and I was mad about it. What I didn't realize, in all my anger, was that I had to FORGIVE.

For almost two years, they did all they could do to destroy me. They tried hard to destroy my reputation and break my spirit, now I had to forgive them. Why? Because my very destiny depended on it. Unforgiveness was preventing me from walking into the fullness of God and into His wonderful plan for my life.

What we fail to realize is that unforgiveness is like drinking poison and expecting the other person to die. Unforgiveness is like being in prison. You are bound by it. The ability to forgive someone who has wronged you creates a sense of peace and freedom. That forgiveness is for us, not the other person.

I finally refused to allow anything and anyone to have that type of power over me. I forgave them and soon I began to see the salvation of the Lord at work. Those individuals who mistreated me were not my problem, and they will never be my problem. I didn't even have a dog in that fight, as the old saying goes.

God's Word is clear: Be not deceived; God is not mocked: for whatsoever a man sow, that shall he also reap (Galatians 6:7). Beloved, never avenge yourselves, but leave the way open for God's wrath; for it is written, 'Vengeance is mine, I will repay', says the Lord (Romans 12:19).

My only requirement was to forgive. I'm telling you this so you will forgive first. Forgive the minute you are wronged. Don't let it fester and get into your mind and spirit. God is a just God and, as my grandmother would always say, "He sits high and He looks low." He sees your struggle, He sees those who have persecuted, used, abused and mistreated you. Pray for them. They need your prayers.

Notice God's salvation did not come until after I forgave. Why, you might ask? Because God's Word is clear in Mark 11:25: Whenever you stand praying, if you have anything against anyone, forgive him so that your Father who is in heaven will also forgive you your transgressions and wrongdoings.

Although I had done everything else God had instructed me to do, I did not begin to see the blessings on the other side until I forgave. Even during the persecution, I had to forgive. When I did, what happened next amazed even me—I began to see their frustration. I could go into meetings where they would attempt to belittle me, and I would smile at them. They no longer had power over me. Forgiveness had broken my chains and released me from prison. I wasn't being arrogant, although that's what I was being called; I was walking in the fullness of God. God was fighting His battle. Remember, it was never my fight anyway.

Like David (in the Bible), I began to remember how He had delivered me from a lion, He had delivered me from a bear, and now he was delivering me from this "uncircumcised Philistine" (1 Samuel 17:36). I began to rest in the Lord. I was moving to the other side. God was aligning people, places and things and it was becoming clear that what the devil meant for bad, God meant for good. I was so at peace that I began to feel sorry for them, knowing they would indeed reap what they were sowing. I prayed heartily for them... And still do.

Forgive Them!!!

CHAPTER 10

Expectation Praise

Once those chains of unforgiveness were broken, I could lift my voice in PRAISE. I began to praise God like never before. I began to praise God for the full manifestation; although I had not received it yet, just knowing it was on the way was enough for me. Have you ever heard "don't wait until the battle is over, shout now?" There's power in that 'expectation praise'. Learn to praise God during the wait! Praise Him in the storm (smile).

What do I mean by 'expectation praise'? Remember how excited we got when our parents told us they were going to take us somewhere or buy us something? We thanked them; told all our friends what good parents we had; sometimes we were so full of excitement and expectation we couldn't even sleep. We did all of this "expecting" they were going to do what they said.

Belief in Santa Claus is another example. We told him what we wanted for Christmas and fully "expected" him to bring it to us. Every day at school we talked about what Santa Claus was bringing us. We'd try to sit up all night Christmas Eve waiting for his arrival. It's the same concept. God tells us what He will do for us in His word (The Bible); however, we don't exhibit that same excitement and expectation when it comes to His promises. When it comes to God, we tend to take a "wait and see" approach. We'll trust our parents and Santa Claus faster than we will trust God.

'Expectation praise' means to praise God while you wait for His promise to manifest, in full expectation trusting that it will indeed happen.

I fooled around and walked into 'expectation praise' and God did exceedingly, abundantly above all I could ask or think. He blessed me in ways I never even dreamed, He opened doors I had not even considered in my wildest dreams, He thrust me years ahead and it became apparent that my latter rain would be greater than my former rain. He did all of that and… gave me a peace that surpasses all understanding.

AND… He did it immediately and suddenly.

Praise Him!!!

CHAPTER 11

The Anointing of Ease

A few months after this ordeal was over, I was watching TV and heard a sermon about the "Anointing of Ease". I don't remember the name of the minister but I remember him talking about Ruth (in the Bible). For those of you who are not familiar with the story of Ruth, let me give a summary.

Ruth was Naomi's daughter-in-law. Naomi lost her husband and two sons. After their deaths, she instructed her two daughters-in-law to return to their respectively families. One daughter-in-law returned home to her family but her other daughter-in-law,

Ruth stayed with Naomi. Ruth vowed to stay and take care of Naomi. Times were very hard for the two of them. Ruth traveled with Naomi to a relative's home. That relative was a very rich farm owner named Boaz. Naomi's plan was to work in the fields, going behind the workers picking up what they left behind and keeping it so she and Naomi could have food. Before long, Boaz noticed Ruth and instructed his worker to purposefully leave handfuls of wheat for Ruth to pick-up. It was "easy" for Ruth. She didn't have to pick anything, only pick-up the piles left behind for her. Ruth was walking in an anointing of ease.

Ruth and Boaz fell in love and married. Ruth went from picking up leftover wheat in a field to owning the entire field.

I, like Ruth, am experiencing an "anointing of ease". If you'd told me a year ago I would be where I am today I would have thought you were crazy. I am an author, business owner, and grandmother who is happy, healthy, financially free, stress-free and enjoying life to its fullest. God has given me beauty for my ashes.

Bear in mind, it was never God's intent for us to live here on earth and have to struggle. But, because of sin and disobedience, living here on earth has become increasingly difficult. Despite our difficulties and challenges please know that God's original plan for mankind still remains, and we have the power to activate it.

Here are the keys:

- Trust in God - Proverbs 3: 5-6

- Have Faith in God - Mark 11:22-24

- Listen to God - Hebrews 12:25

- Obey God - James 1:22-25

- Be Still and know that He is God - Psalm 46:10-11

- Forgive - Mark 11:25-26

- Praise - Luke 24:50-53

Walk in Victory!!!!

CHAPTER 12

The Other Side

I felt betrayed by a company I had given my all. I worked hard supervising my staff, making sure they had the tools they needed to succeed. I worked hard making sure quotas were met and audits were passed. Not just simple mediocre audits, but audits that would have cost that company millions in revenue had those audits gone badly. I was doing everything I was supposed to do and so much more—that is the story of a lot of people in my situation.

I'd work hard to help initiate programs, only to be looked over for promotion and other individuals placed over the programs. I was referred to as a "leader" and then instructed to help train my supervisor, someone hired for a position I'd applied for. I didn't understand it, but it was not for me to understand their "why".   All I had to do was trust God's process.

Those in authority over me did their very best to make my life a living hell, break and destroy me. They schemed, plotted and planned ways to get rid of me or make me quit. They wanted me to feel unworthy and like a failure. Their plans may have succeeded except for the fact I knew I was a child of the most high God, and God didn't make junk.

I heard a Pastor explain once how in the book of Genesis when God created the heavens and the earth, He spoke everything into existence. But, when He made man, God used His hands. We are the only thing God put His hands on. That means we are very important to God. And the way I see it, if I'm important to God, there is no way you can every make me feel inferior and unimportant. Like I said, God doesn't make junk.

In spite of how they tried to make me feel inferior, unlearned, and incompetent, I remembered how many times my expertise had gotten them through those tough audits; I remembered how many employees I'd helped improve their performance; I even remembered how they'd bragged about my knowledge and skills to their superiors. Oh yes, there was a time when they thought I was the best thing since sliced bread. One of them even referred to me as the "smartest person" she knew.   I'd even listened to how they told me what a "leader" I was and how well I knew the job as they charged me with helping the person they hired to supervise me "get up to speed"—even though I'd applied for the job and was told I wasn't qualified.

So, how was I now such an incompetent employee who, as they would often say, "should be glad we gave you a job"?   If they believed me to be the smartest person they knew, what would possibly make them think I wouldn't be smart enough to see this for what it was?   Well, since my smart is holistic (LOL), I did indeed see it for what it was. Especially since I'd only begun to be referred to as incompetent when I spoke out against their unfairness and biases.

As a parent, we love our children and will go out of our way to ensure their safety and security to the best of our ability, although our ability is limited.   Well God's ability is limitless, and just like us parents, He will ensure our safety and security—but on a much higher level.

I'll say it again, what the enemy meant for my bad, God meant for my good. That "set-back" they had planned for me all those years didn't align with what God had to say about it, and My God has the final say in *all* matters concerning me. What I didn't realize at the time was that God was working behind the scenes on something that would blow my mind.

Every verbal attack, every write-up, every demeaning comment, every threat, every set-up devised by them, strengthened me and drew me closer to God and my God-given destiny. It's a fact that our enemies will cause us to be promoted faster than our friends. An enemy can either intimidate you or inspire you, the choice is yours. Mine inspired me. As a matter of fact, they still do.

A few days after leaving that organization, one of its employees, who just happened to be close to my previous supervisor, was noted viewing my LinkedIn professional profile online. For those of you who are not familiar with LinkedIn, it is a business and employment-oriented service that operates via websites and mobile apps. It's mainly used for professional networking. I reached out to this individual to inquire as to why he was inquiring into my professional profile. He responded nervously (he didn't know I could see who had viewed my profile) by stating he and several of the other employees were "worried" about me and hoped I was "ok".

During my tenure there, we were cordial but not friends. I would have been puzzled by his statement had I not been familiar with the nature of my previous supervisor. She was very intimidated by the success of others and experienced individuals caused her a great deal of discomfort. Once she set her sights on you, she would do everything in her power to get rid of you. I'm not telling you what I heard, I'm telling you what I know. I'd been present in many conversations where she talked about other staff members. She made it known when she wanted to get rid of someone and she would do everything in her power to dig up whatever she could on that person; get others to complain about that person; and scheme and plot their demise. Once she'd gotten what she wanted she would then relish in how that person would struggle to find other employment. Her favorite saying was, "If she gets something else, she will never make the kind of money she was making here. She was well paid." Her other favorite saying was, "It's time for her to move on."

Most of the individuals she set her sights on had years of experience and expertise she did not possess. She felt threatened by them and would always try to attack their knowledge base and/or work ethic claiming they were incompetent or they were not doing their jobs. Sound familiar? I have no doubt, she's said these things to others about me as well, especially since she felt so comfortable talking about other employees to me. I thank God for her and all the others I've encountered like her. She never intimidated me but she has inspired me. She inspired me to be all I could be and reach new heights in my personal and professional life.

The climate around her was one of "its ok for you to get ahead, just don't get ahead of me". She'd once informed me that I was highly thought of and admired by my peers as well as by several high-ranking officials in the company. This however was not presented in a congratulatory fashion and, as I later discovered, lead to my being excluded from meetings and conversations that were beneficial to my being able to do my job efficiently and effectively. I was undermined to make me look incompetent due to her lack of confidence and insecurity.

What they didn't realize was that I am a child of the most high God and God always causes me to triumph. Not only did I find other employment, I found it immediately. Not only did I make the money I made there, I made substantially more money doing fewer jobs and not supervising anyone. I'm surrounded by leadership that is fair and unbiased. I'm surrounded by leadership that encourages my growth, and values my expertise and experience. Learning opportunities and opportunities to secure certifications and continued education are not withheld. The leadership at my current company does not take all the business trips and come back to teach the others like my former employer did. We all have the same opportunity to learn and grow. There is a climate of inclusiveness and I can now see myself thriving personally and professionally.

All test and trials are not meant to defeat us, many are sent to stretch us. Stay the course and it will lead you to the will of God. You will never realize how powerful you really are without these tests and trials, and you will never truly realize the power of God in your life without them.

What I didn't realize is that the betrayal I viewed as a "set-back" was a "set-up" to get me to my destiny. Had they not treated me the way they did I would not have moved on. I would have been stuck in a dead-end job not maximizing my fullest potential, surrounded by unhappy, insecure individuals with axes to grind who wholeheartedly hope for my failure. But with my God, failure is not an option. In fact, failure is utterly impossible. I am neither under their feet nor in their hands. I'm in the palm of God's hand surrounded by protection and provision, so they were wasting their time.

As they hope for my failure, I pray for their success. God's Word is true: Whatsoever a man sows he must also reap.

Simply put, you get what you put out. It's scary to think they will get what they put out. But, as scary as it is, it's not my responsibility. We cannot control how others treat us but we can control how we react as well as how we treat them in return. God is the only One who can change a heart. A dirty heart will remain dirty until the individual repents and asks God to come into their heart. All I can do is pray this happens.

I'm on the other side of the affliction. The Bible tells us in Psalm 34:19, "Many are the afflictions of the righteous; but the Lord delivereth him out of them all." The Bible didn't say some; it said all. God delivered me from that situation. And God will deliver you as well.

You, as a child of God, win *all* the time. The Bible also tells us "fret not because of evildoers, neither be thou envious against the workers of iniquity. For they shall soon be cut down like the grass, and wither as the green herb" (Psalm 37: 1-2). This passage of scripture goes on to say in verses 3 – 11 how we are to rest in, trust in and wait on the Lord; we are not to do evil but to cease from anger and wrath, because in a little while those evildoers will be cut off and those who have waited on the Lord will inherit the earth. WE will inherit the earth.

Since the Bible also tells us that "The earth is the Lord's and the fullness thereof; the world, and all that dwells in it" (Psalm 24:1), that's a pretty big inheritance (LOL). It means our Father God will give us the whole world, everything and everybody. And, since God is the God of abundance, don't expect to have what you had before the hard times. You can count on at least double for your trouble. I got everything they tried to keep from me and so much more.

I'm on the other side; the other side of the turmoil. "Turmoil" is defined as *a state of great disturbance, confusion, or uncertainty*. I no longer have to deal with tumultuous individuals plotting and scheming against me so heavily it required they walk back and forth all day between offices (Whoa! That devil going to fro like a hungry lion seeking whom he may devour just came to mind here), closing doors, and scheduling impromptu meetings designed to intimidate and belittle me. You know the ones.   Those meetings where they surround you on all sides with one individual doing all the talking, one individual assign to "read" your expressions; and one there to give the illusion of sympathy for your plight (usually a Human Resources representative), yeah, those kind!

Let's not forget the file folders, they bring to those meetings. Those folders whose contents never seem to be revealed regardless how many questions you ask regarding the allegations they brought you into this meeting to discuss (LOL). I thank God, He always revealed their intent and I was never caught by surprise. He whispered these words into my spirit when I entered the very first meeting "confounded and confused". I didn't realize what it meant at the time but as the meeting unfolded I did. The turmoil was always theirs. As I stated in an earlier chapter, God had already prepared me for those pop-up meetings and attacks. They left those meetings disturbed, confused and uncertain (in turmoil).

I can recall vividly how I was leaving that meeting when one of them turned to the other and asked, "What just happened here?"   I so wanted to turn around and say, "The Power of God just happened here." Instead I just thanked God for His protection and their confusion. Their desire to get rid of me often trumped reasonable behavior, and their interactions with me would often turn into personal attacks, especially if I'd ask what they viewed as "too many questions"; especially "too many questions" for which they had no answers. It was obvious I was far more irritating than irritated.

The Bible tells us that wisdom is the main thing and we should get wisdom, but it also instructs us that while getting the wisdom we should also get understanding (Proverbs 4:7). I really don't think they asked God for either (LOL).

I can only imagine how many of you have experienced the same or similar incidents on your jobs. Unfortunately, this seems all too common. As I was going through this ordeal, I would reach out to friends and family for emotional support. Time and time again I would hear countless stories of how they too had been treated unfairly and discriminated against on various jobs. It didn't matter whether they worked in the kitchen or in upper-level management, the stories all described the same type of treatment and behavior by their superiors. The only difference is how they each reacted.

Some, usually those in the lower paying jobs, felt they had to endure the unfair treatment because they needed their jobs. They felt that if they said anything that made waves, they would be retaliated against and fired. They felt trapped because they believed they lacked the education and or skills to secure employment elsewhere; and many of them were single parents at the time.

Others complained about the unfair treatment and were retaliated against so heavily that working for the company became so unbearable they quit and sought employment elsewhere. Although retaliatory behavior against a person or persons making a complaint of discrimination is illegal, companies still do it. It may be under the guise of disciplinary action based on alleged complaints by others; it may be through exclusions (they forget to send you a meeting invite for a very important meeting; your name is 'accidentally' left off an email for a request for information and you are later written up for not having provided the information, etc.).

There are many games they will play. However, once you have filed formal charges with the Equal Employment Opportunity Commission (EEOC), you do have recourse if they retaliate. You can file retaliation charges with the EEOC each and every time they exhibit retaliatory behavior against you. I'm not a lawyer and cannot offer legal advice, but I do suggest you seek legal counsel should you find yourself in this situation.

Unfortunately, very few of the individuals I spoke with filed formal complaints with their companies and/or the EEOC; and unfortunately not doing so allowed the individual(s) and/or companies to continue this behavior without any recourse or intervention. Often, the behavior becomes business as usual and they move on, discriminating against the next person, and so on and so on.

If you are being treated unfairly, discriminated against, experiencing retaliatory behavior, and/or being harassed on your job, pray and ask God for guidance.

If you decide to move forward with any type of allegation against your workplace, you may face retaliatory behavior like the individuals I spoke with. The EEOC prefers, if possible, you reach out to the company's Human Resource or Compliance Department first. You always need to give the company an opportunity to correct any issues internally first. If you don't do so, the company can later claim they had no knowledge there was a problem and had they known, would have worked to correct the issue. Some companies will work hard, once notified, to ensure you are treated fairly and your allegations are addressed appropriately without recourse or retaliation.

Also, once you've made a formal complaint and retaliatory behavior begin, you can also make a formal complaint regarding the retaliatory behavior. Make sure you follow through reporting each incidence of retaliatory behavior every time you are retaliated against.

I know some of you have heard the phrase "Location, Location, Location" when it comes to selling and buying real estate. Well, when it comes to workplace bias, discrimination, retaliation, and/or harassment I say DOCUMENT, DOCUMENT, DOCUMENT.

Document who, what, when, and where:

- Who committed the act as well as who else was present when the act was committed;

- What was said or done (document as much detail as possible and be very specific);

- When it occurred (precise date and time);

- Where it occurred (private office, break-room, bathroom, etc., be specific).

Another very important step is to make sure you recap *all* meetings, such as the one I described above, in a follow-up email to all meeting participants. Be sure to send this email utilizing a "read receipt". They don't have to respond to your email, and most times they won't, you just need to know they read it.

Send "follow-up" and "clarification" emails for any interactions or exchanges between yourself and the employer, as well as between yourself and your subordinates, especially when there have been reports that your subordinates are making complaints against you to your employer.

If you've never been a note taker, you might want to start. You'll thank me later, especially if you ever find yourself in this situation.

I know of some individuals who used recording devices when meeting with their superiors but I don't recommend this. I will say this again, I am not a lawyer therefore I am not offering legal advice. I just personally don't recommend using recording devices. That's why you need to take good notes, especially if you don't have a good memory.

Be mindful that your employer may try to convince you that you are overreacting and there are no grounds for your allegations. Some may even go so far as to try and place a guilt trip on you with statements like, "How could you think we would do such a thing?" "It really hurts us that you don't trust us."

Problem is, if it looks like a duck; quacks like a duck; and acts like a duck, it's usually a duck. If it causes you discomfort and something is not sitting well with you, it warrants investigation regardless what anyone else thinks. And, you are well within your rights to make your concerns known.

Also, be mindful of your peers. What I find odd is how individuals in your same situation   try to deter you from making a formal complaint; turn their backs on you if you do; and even report your every move to your employer.   Your willingness to step up will not only benefit you but will also benefit them. But, on the other hand you don't want people in your boat poking holes and/or rowing in the opposite direction. Everyone who lends a so-called 'sympathetic ear', agreeing with you, and even sharing their own stories of discrimination is not with you. Some of them will even throw you under the bus and back over you when things get hot.

God will send who you need. Trust His process and leave some people where they are. Remember you can't share everything with everyone. Ask God for a spirit of discernment so you will see the intentions of those around you.

However, don't make the mistake of not praying for God to also guard your heart in the process. Who and what He shows you can often hurt you to your very core. That person you thought you could trust just might be the person telling your employer your every move. You don't have time to waste being hurt by that. You have a far greater mission. You need to be able to shake that dust from your feet and keep it moving.

My next suggestion is pray, pray, and pray. I've outlined the steps, in previous chapters, aimed at helping you get to the other side of this type of dilemma. However, I cannot stress enough, the importance of having a firm and consistent relationship with God at this juncture in your life.

Pray without ceasing. God will guide you through the process and He will deliver you safely on the other side. You will have gone through a fire and won't even smell like smoke. Don't look back!

CHAPTER 13

Better, Not Bitter

I never thought I would say "I'm better, not bitter." It was hard for me to imagine, after all they put me through, that I would not harbor even the slightest ill-will toward them, but surprisingly I don't. I wish them well. I would like to take this time to thank them. Hopefully they are reading this book, and even better they paid for it (LOL).

If they are reading this I would like to say... I truly thank you for being the cruel, unjust and unfair individuals you were. You forced upon me a strength I never knew existed in me; you caused me to walk into my destiny; you caused me to live an abundant life; you caused me to know without a shadow of doubt, if God be for me, no one can be against me and no weapon ever formed against me will prosper. Again, thank you!!!

I'm reminded of the story of Joseph (Genesis 37-50). Joseph was favored by his father because of the father's love for Joseph's mother. Joseph's brothers knew their father loved Joseph more than them, which caused them to hate Joseph (Genesis 37:3). Joseph also possessed a gift—he was a dreamer. And to make matters worse, Joseph started telling his brothers about his dreams; dreams where he was a ruler over them (Genesis 37:5-11). This only angered his brothers more. Joseph's brothers soon began plotting to kill him. One of his brothers objected to killing him and suggested they throw Joseph into a pit. That brother planned to come back later and rescue Joseph, but before he was able to do so the other brothers sold Joseph into slavery when a caravan of merchants passed by. The brothers then took Joseph's robe, dipped it in animal blood and returned to their father saying that Joseph had been killed by a wild animal (Genesis 37: 18-35).

The merchants later sold Joseph to a man named Potiphar—a high-ranking Egyptian. Even in Joseph's dire situation, as a slave, God caused him to find favor with Potiphar. No worries, no matter what your situation may look like and no matter who or what is coming against you, God will bring people into your life, line up events and provide resources that are critical to you reaching your destiny.

God caused Joseph to prosper right where he was. Potiphar could see how Joseph excelled at his duties and Joseph became one of his most trusted servants, causing Potiphar to put Joseph in charge of his household. High-ranking officials on your job will see you excel as well, even when others are coming against you and/or lying on you telling them you are not doing your job, or you don't have what it takes to get that promotion.

Joseph was heading toward his destiny—the one in his dreams where he saw himself as a ruler. You guessed it. The devil had to step in. Remember he's here to kill, still and destroy. Steal hopes and desires, kill dreams, and destroy destinies before they manifest in the earth in the fullness of God according to God's word.

He (the devil) couldn't stand by and let Joseph reach his destiny without a fight. So, he (the devil) stepped in and caused Potiphar's wife to falsely accuse Joseph. Her accusation caused Potiphar to place his most trusted servant in prison (Genesis 39:7-20). Even in prison, God was with Joseph (Genesis 39:21-23). While in prison, Joseph interpreted a dream for a fellow prisoner who turned out to be the king's cupbearer. This prisoner was later released and when the king began having troubling dreams of his own, this former prisoner remembered Joseph and his gift for dream interpretation. Joseph was released from prison to interpret the king's dream.

Based on Pharaoh's dream, Joseph predicted seven years of bountiful harvest followed by seven years of severe famine in Egypt and advised the king to begin storing grain in preparation for this famine (Genesis 41:1-37). Because of Joseph's wisdom, the king made Joseph a ruler in Egypt, second only to the king. I guess you could say Joseph went from PIT to PALACE. There's that Jeremiah 29:11 blessing again. Joseph oversaw food storage during the seven years of plenty and in charge of selling grain to Egyptians and foreigners during the seven years of famine (Genesis 41:38-57).

What his brothers meant for bad, so many years earlier, God meant for good. Fortunately for us, another's wrong doing cannot trump our doing the right thing when it comes to us reaching our destiny. No matter what someone does to us and how hard they try to destroy us, if we continue to do what is right and walk upright before God, they cannot steal our God-given destiny.   In other words, if we are divinely aligned with God, our divine alignment will override a person's desire to keep us down. They have absolutely no control over us or our destiny.

As destiny would have it, the famine reached Canaan and Joseph's family (his father and brothers) were affected. His brothers, except for his younger brother Benjamin, traveled to Egypt to purchase grain. When they arrived, and sat before Joseph, they did not recognize him, but he recognized them.   This had to be difficult for Joseph. Seeing his brothers brought back memories of how they plotted his demise all those years ago. Joseph did not retaliate and God allowed him to know his brothers were sorrowful for the way they'd treated him, thereby softening his heart even further towards them.

Joseph even realized God's greater plan. After all his suffering Joseph realized his brothers had not set him on that path, but that it was God all the time. God saw ahead, as He always does, knowing Joseph would need to be in the position he was in at that precise moment in time to save the lives of his people. And just as he'd seen in his dreams, all those years before, his brothers bowed to him fulfilling his previous prophesy (Genesis 43:26).

We sometimes find ourselves in unfair and unjust circumstances such as the ones Joseph faced. However, there is much to be learned from Joseph's story. Joseph remained faithful; he had a willingness to submit and obey God; he was divinely aligned therefore he could walk in his divine destiny.

By remaining faithful and accepting that God is ultimately in charge, we can be confident that God will reward our faithfulness. Man's most wicked intentions towards us can never override the perfect will of God for us. But, we must remain properly aligned with God. Not even our own foolishness can override the perfect will of God.

What do I mean? Look at Joseph. There he was a teenager, whose brothers were already jealous and envious of him, who told his brothers he had a dream where he saw them bowing to him. If that's not foolishness, I don't know what is (LOL).

When the lady in the parking lot of Bath and Body Works provided the answer to the question I'd asked God days before, I knew I was in proper alignment. Alignment is defined as an arrangement in a straight line or in correct or appropriate relative positions; a position of agreement or alliance. I was in the appropriate position to get to my destiny—that place where God had all my blessings waiting for me. The very thing the devil was trying to hide from me, with all those distractions, was apparent. This difficulty I was facing was not about me. As a matter of fact, it was bigger than me.

God had a plan; a Jeremiah 29:11 kind of plan. A plan to prosper me, give me hope and a future. Once again that is why the devil was working so hard to throw me off course and get me out of alignment. He didn't want me to have an alliance (union, affiliation, partnership) with God. He knew God was going to do exceedingly and abundantly in my life more than I could have ever imagined or asked for. He'd (the devil) failed, just like the employers he sent to distract me.

When I look at those who mistreated me, I know they were mere pawns in the devil's game. He used them and they allowed themselves to be used. Everything they did, they meant for my bad. But, God turned it all around and made it all work in my favor. Therefore, I don't harbor any ill-will toward them.

You shouldn't harbor ill-will toward those who have persecuted you and done you wrong. The Bible tells us that we are more than conquerors (Romans 8:37). Not just conquerors, but *more* than conquerors. The dictionary defines conqueror as one who wins in a war; overcomes an adversary; defeat; vanquish; overwhelm; crush; squash; trounce. After reading this definition I really felt sorry for them knowing they allowed themselves to be used by the devil. They decided to play on the losing team. God's people *always* win. We are BORN TO WIN.

When we accept Christ as our Savior and enter fellowship and alliance with God, we can't lose. Therefore, it is so important to know which side you are on—God's or the devil. That is also why we don't fall into the devil's trap by harboring ill-will, hatred and malice in our hearts against those who mistreat us. Doing so will mess up our alignment.

I know you've heard the saying "we don't forgive people for them, we forgive people for us". This statement could not be truer. Forgiveness sets us free not them. Repentance sets them free.

The lies my employer told and the plots they plotted went against the very nature of God, but were in total alignment with the nature of the devil. The very nature of the devil is that of deception. And, since we know who won the fight for our salvation, we need not concern ourselves with those who come against us.

We need only pray for them; pray they decide to fight on the winning team someday—God's team.

You are all that and a bag of chips!

CHAPTER 14

I Made It, And So Will You!

As I talked about in the previous chapter, Joseph's journey took many years. My journey took a mere two years and it felt like a lifetime. The Bible tells us "God was with Joseph" and I don't doubt that was how Joseph was able to make it. I don't doubt that was how I was able to make it; and I don't doubt that is how you will be able to make it as well.

If you're unsure as to if you are in divine alignment with God, ask Him. We often make things harder than they should be. Go to God in prayer, with a pure heart and intent to please God and do His will. God will make His will clear to you. Just like He used a lady in the parking lot of a Bath and Body Works to let me know I was in proper alignment with His will for me, He'll reveal His perfect will for you. We have not, because we ask not. We'll go to everybody and their mother to find out what God's will is for us, but we won't ask God.

Let me caution you, His will for you may not be what you want and walking contrary to His will causes you to be out of alignment. He won't desert you but you won't live your best life. Think about it like this: although an automobile may be out of proper alignment it still functions. It gets us from point A to point B. Problem is that it doesn't get us there in the smooth and economical fashion in which it was designed to. The ride is bumpier and our tires wear out faster costing us money. In other words, being out of alignment with God will cause you to have a bumpy ride and cost you money (LOL).

Let's look at Jonah for a minute. For those of you who don't know the story of Jonah, Jonah was an Israelite whom God had called to be a prophet. Jonah refused to accept his divine mission and left on a sea voyage instead. He was running from God and his divine calling. God had instructed Jonah to go to a city called Nineveh and preach there because the people were very wicked, but Jonah decided to go the opposite direction to a city called Tarsish.

Well, God sent a huge storm and the ship Jonah was on was in danger of sinking. Jonah knew he had disobeyed God and God was angry with him. He was the blame for this storm and was putting the other men on the ship in danger. Once the men on the ship realized what was going on, although reluctant, they threw Jonah overboard in the storm. As soon as they threw him overboard the storm stopped.

Even though Jonah had disobeyed God, God was still merciful towards him. Instead of allowing Jonah to drown God caused a whale to swallow Jonah. Jonah stayed inside the whale for three days. He was out of alignment with God therefore his road was bumpy and cost him money (LOL). I'm sure Jonah was unable to work those three days and his lodging wasn't the best. While inside the whale, Jonah began to pray and ask God for forgiveness; and after three days, the whale spit Jonah out onto dry land.

God is the God of second chances. He is even the God of third, fourth, and fifth chances, but it is up to us to ask for the chance. We don't always get it right the first time. As a matter of fact, I started this book off by saying I spent far too much time fighting a fight that wasn't mine. It really doesn't matter how you start or even what happens in between; what matters is how you finish. I have a desire to do great things and finish well, finish strong. It is my desire that each of you finish well and finish strong, too.

Stay the course and know that God loves you. He desires only the best for you. He didn't make junk when he made you. You always win and no matter what people call you, the only thing that matters is what you answer to.

Whose report will you believe? I suggest you believe the report of the Lord. We are quick to say, "I'm not letting anyone talk to me like that" when we should actually be saying, "I'm not letting anyone talk about me like that."

What I mean is don't allow anyone to speak negatively about you to your spirit. When someone, I don't care who it is, tells you that you are dumb, unworthy, unintelligent, ugly, whatever they've said to belittle you, you look them square in the eye and say, "I am none of those things. God spoke the heavens and earth into existence, but He took the time to make *me* with His hands—and God doesn't make junk!"

BE STILL! God has your back. He has an amazing life in store for you. Just tie a knot in your rope and hold on.

"And let us not grow weary while doing good, for in due season we shall reap if we do not lose heart." (Galatians 6:9, NKJV)

~ The End ~

Acknowledgments

I would like to dedicate this book to my husband, John. The one, who saw me in my most vulnerable, bruised and battered state, loved me and loved me hard. His love and support is one of the biggest reasons I made it through, although I knew sometimes he felt helpless and wished he could simply "fix-it".

To my Mom and Dad, who taught me to stand up for what is right knowing that only right will stand, and for praying for and encouraging me through it all. You better believe a "Praying Mother" is a force to be reckoned with (LOL).

To Tammy, for talking me off many ledges during this ordeal and helping me maintain my sanity.

To those employees and co-workers who stood with me, encouraged me, supported me and prayed for me.

To all my prayer partners who answered my call to action and undergirded me.

To Sherry, who was able to capture the essence of BE STILL AND KNOW with a camera.

To Jamie, for your creative expertise and allowing God to speak to you while teaching me how to heal.

To Vicki, for your selfless act of sharing.

To R.C. and C. D., for your guidance and support.

WE DID IT!!!

ALL Glory and Honor goes to GOD for providing the divine connections required for me to get through that ordeal and walk in my divine purpose. The best is yet to come!!!

With Love,

About the Author

Dena Richard is a fresh and upcoming author who resides in Pleasant Grove, Alabama. In 1986, she began her career as a Registered Nurse and quickly realized her passion was caring for critically ill patients.

Although she no longer serves as a traditional "bedside nurse", her nursing career spans three decades and she is currently employed as a Registered Nurse Clinical Compliance Auditor.

"Be Still and Know" is her first book. Over the years and after many experiences, she has become a champion for the underdog fighting against injustice and discrimination, especially in the workplace. Dena has been married to John Richard for 29 years, and they have two wonderful sons, Gabriel and Ephraim. They also have a granddaughter, Reagan, who is the apple of their eye.

Made in the USA
Columbia, SC
19 July 2019